APPLIQUÉ
MASTERPIECE

Affairs
of the
Heart

AIE ROSSMANN

American Quilter's Society
P. O. Box 3290 • Paducah, KY 42002-3290
www.americanquilter.com

Located in Paducah, Kentucky, the American Quilter's Society (AQS) is dedicated to promoting the accomplishments of today's quilters. Through its publications and events, AQS strives to honor today's quilt-makers and their work and to inspire future creativity and innovation in quiltmaking.

EDITOR: BARBARA SMITH
GRAPHIC DESIGN: ELAINE WILSON
COVER DESIGN: MICHAEL BUCKINGHAM
PHOTOGRAPHY: CHARLES R. LYNCH

Library of Congress Cataloging-in-Publication Data
Rossmann, Aie
    Appliqué materpiece. Affairs of the heart / by Aie Rossmann.
        p.cm.
    ISBN 1-57432-859-X
    1. Appliqué--Patterns. 2. Quilting--Patterns. 3. Patchwork--Patterns. 4. Heart in art. I. Title: Affairs of the heart. II. Title.

    TT779.R68 2004
    746.44'5041--dc22

                            2004012598

Additional copies of this book may be ordered from:
American Quilter's Society, PO Box 3290, Paducah, KY 42002-3290;
800-626-5420 (orders only please); or online at
www.americanquilter.com. For all other inquiries, call 270-898-7903.

Pluck this little flower and take it, delay not! I fear lest it droop and drop into the dust.

It may not find a place in thy garland, but honour it with a touch of pain from thy hand and pluck it. I fear lest the day end before I am aware, and the time of offering go by.

Though its colour be not deep and its smell be faint, use this flower in thy service and pluck it while there is time.

Rabindranath Tagore

AFFAIRS OF THE HEART, 62" x 62", made by the author

Contents

Introduction

When I started teaching needle-turn appliqué, heart motifs quickly became a favorite of mine. They are easy to appliqué, yet still look absolutely charming in quilts. AFFAIRS OF THE HEART has 36 appliquéd blocks, each containing a heart motif. The blocks are easy enough to be tackled by novices with basic appliqué skills, yet they are intricate in appearance and will keep even the experts engaged. The blocks are also of a manageable size, so each one can be completed in a single sitting.

While I made my quilt by hand with the needle-turn method, the designs lend themselves to other appliqué techniques and could easily be sewn by machine. The border and one of the appliqué blocks are done in reverse appliqué, whereby the background fabric, which is on top, is cut through to reveal the colored fabric pieces below. Each of the blocks also contains embroidered embellishments, which are quite simply done by hand with a stem stitch. If you prefer, they can be sewn with the decorative stitches many sewing machines are capable of producing.

General Instructions

The blocks in the AFFAIRS OF THE HEART wallhanging are straight-set in six rows of six. Of course, there are many ways these blocks can be used, either singly or in combination, to make numerous quilt projects.

Fabric Selection

For this quilt, it is essential to have a large variety of 100 percent cotton fabric scraps in different colors and values from which to select appliqué pieces. Large pieces of fabric are not needed, because only a few appliqué pieces will be cut from any particular fabric. Building up a diverse collection of appliqué fabrics, therefore, does not have to be particularly costly. My collection ranges from tiny scraps to fat quarters. I seldom have any piece large enough in my stash for background or backing because these are typically custom-bought for each quilt.

BLOCKS. This quilt might appear to be made mostly with hand-dyes and batiks, but in actual fact, it also has many different kinds of commercial fabrics, including geometrics and florals, and both large and small commercial prints. In particular, I find that commercial fabrics with large prints provide an economical way to create variety. A piece of such fabric will have many different colors and values, and small appliqué pieces can be selectively cut from within a large print. Using a variety of fabrics gives more depth to a design and makes a quilt seem more vibrant and alive. I find that it is best to use tightly woven fabrics, such as batiks, because they are less likely to fray than looser weaves.

NARROW BORDERS. If you look at the quilt photo on page 4, you will see that the three narrow borders are cut from a fabric printed with scallops. A stripe or other print would also look attractive.

WIDE BORDER. Yardage and instructions are given for a wide border that is reverse appliquéd, requiring two fabrics. There is also an appliqué heart pattern in each corner of the quilt.

Fabric Requirements

Finished quilt: 62" x 62"

Finished blocks: 7" x 7"

All yardage requirements are based on fabric at least 42" wide. Use 100 percent cotton for best results. Extra yardage is included for prewash shrinkage and minor cutting errors.

Fabric	Yards
Assorted scraps for appliqué	—
Black background squares	2½
Narrow borders	1
Wide border, black	2
Wide border, multicolored	2
Binding	⅝
Sashing	⅛
Backing	4

Supplies

* Batting (cotton), 66" x 66"

* Embroidery floss, 7 skeins yellow or gold

* Dressmaker's tracing paper, 5 sheets 18" x 24"

* Ballpoint pen for tracing appliqué designs (use pen on paper only)

* Fabric marking pencils or pens

* 100 percent cotton thread, 50 weight/3 ply, for piecing

* 100 percent cotton thread for hand quilting

* Clear and flexible template plastic for appliqué templates

* A fine-point permanent marking pen for drawing on template plastic

* Quilting needles (betweens) for hand quilting

* Appliqué needles (sharps) for hand appliqué

* Needle threader

* Thimble

* Small, pointed, sharp scissors for cutting fabric

* Small, pointed, sharp scissors for cutting template plastic

APPLIQUÉ THREAD. I use many different colors of 50-weight, 3-ply, 100 percent cotton thread for hand appliqué. Many colors are needed because the thread has to match the appliqué fabric. If you have a collection of 60-weight, 2-ply, 100 percent cotton thread (also known as bobbin thread), it can also be used for hand appliqué.

Some quilters use very fine 100 percent silk thread in a neutral color. This thread comes in a variety of values, from light to dark. It can be used for appliquéing fabric with similar values instead of trying to match the colors as you need to do with cotton thread. Fine stitches made with such thread tend to sink into the appliqué pieces and become invisible.

NEEDLES. There are a variety of needles on the market: betweens for hand quilting; and sharps, straws, and appliqué needles for appliqué. I use quilting needles (betweens in size 12) for both hand appliqué and hand quilting. I find it easier to keep my appliqué stitches small with a small needle. Try using a variety of needles and see which type works best for you. The best needle for you depends on both the size of your hand and the way in which you hold the needle.

NEEDLE THREADERS. Needle threaders are quite helpful if you do hand appliqué and hand quilting. Choose a good quality needle threader with a very fine wire loop so that you can pull the thread through the eye of the needle without having to pull so hard that you break the wire loop. A good quality needle threader may cost five to ten times that of an inferior one, but it will save you time and frustration, and it is more economical in the long run.

SCISSORS. It is best to use a rotary cutter and cutting mat to cut the background squares and border strips, but you will need a pair of small, pointed, and very sharp scissors for cutting appliqué pieces. For cutting paper and template plastic you will need another pair of small scissors, so that you don't ruin your fabric scissors on template plastic.

TEMPLATE PLASTIC. I make templates for each appliqué piece from clear, flexible template plastic and a very fine permanent marking pen. Place the template plastic on top of the design and trace the design on the plastic sheet with a pen. When the templates are cut, there is no need to add a seam allowance. Soft template plastic that comes in rolls is easier to work with than the harder more common variety that comes in small sheets.

BASTING PINS. I use appliqué pins for basting small appliqué pieces in place. Run the pins right on the seam line of each appliqué piece and remove them as your appliqué stitches approach the pins. To help keep your thread from catching on the pins, keep the number of pins to a minimum by basting only one piece at a time. After a piece has been appliquéd, remove the pins before pinning the next piece. It is preferable to thread-baste large pieces rather than pin them, as in the reverse appliqué scroll border (pattern begins on page 90).

Fabric Preparation

I do not prewash fabrics used for wallhangings. I think of them as display pieces, like paintings, and keep them clean by minimizing the extent to which they are handled. You can gently vacuum the dust that might accumulate on them rather than wash them. If you prefer to wash and test the dye-fastness and shrinkage of fabrics before using them, then by all means do. In any event, be sure to be consistent in your approach to fabric preparation and to iron all creases out of your fabrics before cutting them.

Cutting Fabrics

Referring to the cutting chart on page 10 and figures 1 and 2, pages 10–11, use a rotary cutter and mat to cut all the background squares. Notice that they are cut 2" wider and longer than the finished block size, because appliqué stitching tends to shrink the background square.

Cutting Chart

Cut from	Required number	Starting size (before appliqué)	Trimmed size (after appliqué)	Finished size (when sewn together)
Background fabric	36 squares	9" x 9"	7½" x 7½"	7" x 7"
Narrow border	4 strips	1½" x 32"	—	1" x 30"
	4 strips	1½" x 48" pieced	—	1" x 46"
	4 strips	1½" x 64" pieced	—	1" x 62"
Wide border fabrics • Black • Multicolored	4 strips each fabric	9" x 64" (length of fabric)	7½" x 62"	7" x 60"
Binding	7 strips	2½" x 42" (width of fabric)	—	—
Sashing	8 strips	1½" x 7½"	—	1" x 7"

Fig. 1. Fabric Cutting Plan for Background Squares. Each square is cut 9" x 9".

Preparing Background Squares

To transfer an appliqué design onto each background square, you will need to make a copy of the block pattern. You can do this by either tracing the pattern on paper or by making a photocopy of the pattern.

Transferring Patterns

1. Fold the background block into quarters to find the center, then finger press the folds.

2. Unfold the block and tape it, right side up, to a hard surface, such as a table.

3. Cut a sheet of dressmaker's tracing paper the same size as the background block. This sheet can be reused for several blocks.

4. Find the center of the tracing paper by folding it into quarters as before.

5. Tape the dressmaker's tracing paper, colored side down, on top of the background block, taking care to align the centers.

6. Tape the appliqué pattern, right side up, on top of the dressmaker's tracing paper and match the pattern's center mark to the center of the tracing paper.

7. Trace the appliqué pattern with a ball-point pen. Make sure that you apply enough pressure for the design to transfer to the background fabric.

8. Once you have finished tracing, remove the pattern sheet and dressmaker's tracing paper from the table. Because the tracings from the dressmaker's tracing paper will rub off easily, go over the design on the background square with a marking pencil.

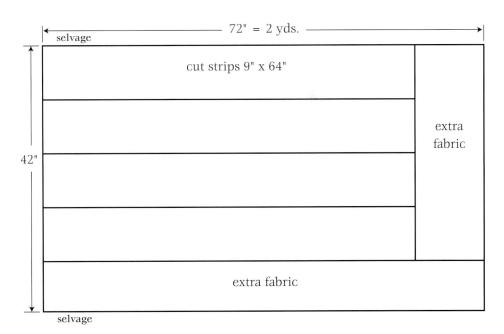

Fig. 2. Fabric Cutting Plan for Scroll Border. Use this diagram to cut both the black and the multicolored wide border fabrics.

Trimming Tips

To trim your blocks, you can use a freezer-paper template the same size as the finished block (7" x 7"). The freezer paper, which can be reused to trim a number of blocks, acts as a stabilizer to keep the blocks from shifting and stretching as they are being cut. This method makes assembling the quilt much easier because the blocks can be precisely trimmed to exactly the same size.

To make sure that the appliqué design of each block will be centered after it is trimmed, the center of the appliquéd block should first be marked by folding it into quarters. Then fold the 7" freezer-paper square into quarters to find its center. Put the appliquéd block, right side down, on an ironing board. Place the freezer-paper square, shiny side down, on top of the appliquéd block and match the centers. Use a hot, dry iron to adhere the freezer paper to the block. Once the freezer-paper template is stuck securely on the block, use a rotary cutter and ruler to trim the block to 7½" x 7½", which allows for a ½" allowance around the freezer paper.

Cutting Templates

1. To make appliqué templates, trace the entire block design onto template plastic with a fine-point, permanent marking pen. Number the templates and cut them out without adding seam allowances.

2. On the right side of the appliqué fabric, trace along template 1 with a marking pencil. Use a white pencil for dark fabrics and a silver pencil for light fabrics. Cut out the appliqué piece ³⁄₁₆" beyond the traced line.

3. Turn under the allowance by finger pressing it. You do not need to turn under any edges that will be overlapped by other pieces.

4. Position the piece on the background square. Pin it to make sure that it is well-aligned on the traced pattern, then appliqué it in place.

5. In the same manner, prepare the rest of the appliqué pieces and appliqué them to the background in numerical order.

6. Add embroidery by using the stem stitch and yellow embroidery floss (fig. 3). Press the work from the back after the appliqué is done.

7. Trim the block to 7½" x 7½", taking great care to ensure that the design is centered on the trimmed block (see Trimming Tips).

right handed

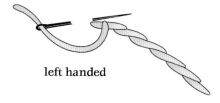

left handed

Fig. 3. Stem stitch

| block 1 | sash | block 2 | block 3 | block 4 | block 5 | block 6 |

sash

| block 7 | block 8 | block 9 | block 10 | block 11 | block 12 |

| block 13 | block 14 | block 15 | block 16 | block 17 | block 18 |

| block 19 | block 20 | block 21 | block 22 | block 23 | block 24 |

| block 25 | block 26 | block 27 | block 28 | block 29 | block 30 |

| block 31 | block 32 | block 33 | block 34 | block 35 | block 36 |

Fig. 4. Quilt assembly. Arrows indicate the direction of seam allowance pressing.

Assembling the Blocks

1. Referring to the photo of the quilt (page 4) and the quilt assembly diagram (fig. 4, page 13), arrange the center blocks into four rows of four each. Sew the blocks together in rows. Then sew the rows together. Press the work from the back.

2. Sew the four 1½" x 32" narrow border strips to the quilt and miter the corners. Press the seam allowances toward the border.

3. Referring to the quilt photo (page 4) and the quilt assembly diagram (page 13), arrange and sew blocks 7, 13, 19, 25 and two 1½" x 7½" sashing strips together. Press seam allowances as shown in the diagram. Sew this strip to the left side of the quilt top.

4. Likewise, arrange and join blocks 12, 18, 24, 30, and two sashing strips. Press seam allowances as shown. Sew this strip to the right side of the quilt.

5. Arrange and sew blocks 2, 3, 4, and 5 together. Add the sashing strips and blocks 1 and 6. Press seam allowances as shown, then sew the strip to the top of the quilt.

6. Arrange and sew blocks 32, 33, 34, 35 together into a strip and add the sashing strips and blocks 31 and 36. Press the seam allowances as shown, then sew the strip to the bottom.

Wide Border (reverse appliqué)

1. Make a copy of the border and corner designs (pages 91–93). You can do this by tracing the patterns on tracing paper or by making photocopies.

2. Cut and tape together sheets of dressmaker's tracing paper to make a border-sized strip 9" x 64". You will be able to use this one strip for all four borders. Find the center of the dressmaker's tracing paper strip by folding it in half crosswise, then lengthwise. On the paper side of the tracing paper, use a pencil to mark two 11" intervals to the right and two 11" intervals to the left of the center line.

3. Fold each border fabric strip, as you did the tracing paper, to find its center. Use a pencil to mark two 11" intervals to the right and two 11" intervals to the left of the center line.

4. Tape a black background border strip, right side up, on a table, and tape the dressmaker's tracing paper, colored side down, on top of the background strip. The border pattern, which should be on top, will be moved from one 11" interval to another as you trace the design. Referring to the quilt photo, place and trace the border design four times on each border strip. Because the chalk lines will brush off easily, go over the lines on the fabric with a pencil.

 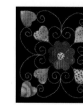  

5. With both fabrics right side up, use a running stitch to baste each multicolored fabric strip underneath each background border strip.

6. Use reverse appliqué to sew the scrolls. When all the appliqué is done, remove any basting stitches and trim away the multicolored fabric from under the background, leaving a ⅜" allowance. Appliqué the circles as indicated on the design. Press the work from the back.

7. Trim each appliquéd border strip to 7½" x 62", making sure that the design is centered on the strips. Wait to appliqué the corner scrolls until after the borders have been sewn to the quilt.

Fig. 5. Place each heart 2½" from the outside corner, and appliqué the solid heart.

Corner Heart (appliqué)

1. Trace the corner heart motif (page 91) on the multicolored fabric. Cut the fabric heart with a ³⁄₁₆" turn-under allowance. Note that the heart should be left as a solid shape for now without trimming away the inside.

2. Appliqué a multicolored heart in each corner of the scroll border, taking care to align the centers of the hearts with the mitered border seams (fig. 5). The edges of the hearts should abut the adjacent scrolls.

3. Once the solid hearts have been appliquéd, reverse appliqué the inside of each heart, revealing the black background fabric (fig. 6). Then add the circles to complete the border (fig. 7, page 16).

Fig. 6. Reverse appliqué the inside of each heart.

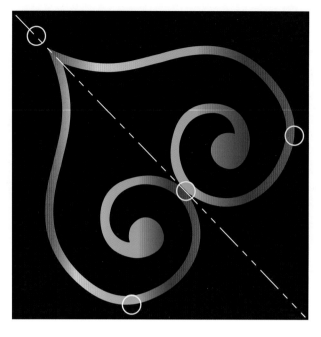

Fig. 7. Add circles.

Attaching Borders

1. Sew a 1½" x 46½" narrow border strip to the inside edge of each wide border, taking care to match their centers.

2. Sew a 1½" x 62½" narrow border strip to the outside edge of each wide border strip, again ensuring that their centers match.

3. Sew these border units to the quilt top and miter the corners. Make sure all seam allowances are pressed according to the quilt assembly diagram.

Finishing the Quilt

1. Cut the backing fabric in half crosswise to form two panels at least 66" long. Sew the panels, right sides together, along one long seam (minus selvages).

2. Layer the quilt top, batting, and backing. Baste the layers together.

3. Quilt the layers. As a suggestion, you can outline quilt around the appliqué designs in the blocks and quilt in the ditch along the border seams. If you have used the scroll pattern in the wide border, it can be echo quilted.

4. Remove all basting and markings when the quilting is completed, and trim the batting and backing even with the quilt top.

5. Use the binding strips to cover the raw edges of the quilt. Enough strips have been included in the cutting chart for any straight-grain binding technique, including double-fold French binding.

6. Make a label and stitch it to the back of your quilt.

Block Patterns

This section contains full-sized patterns for the 36 appliqué blocks. A color photo accompanies each block. The center of each pattern is marked. Be sure to transfer the center mark as you trace each pattern. Embroidery details are marked in red on the patterns.

Block 1

Appliqué Masterpiece: **Affairs of the Heart** *by Aie Rossmann*

Add a ³⁄₁₆" turn-under allowance to each appliqué fabric piece.

Appliqué pieces to the background in numerical order.

Embroidery is shown in red.

Block 2

Add a ¾₁₆" turn-under allowance to each appliqué fabric piece.
Appliqué pieces to the background in numerical order.
Embroidery is shown in red.

Block 3

Appliqué Masterpiece: **Affairs of the Heart** *by Aie Rossmann*

Add a ³⁄₁₆" turn-under allowance to each appliqué fabric piece.

Appliqué pieces to the background in numerical order.

Embroidery is shown in red.

Block 4

Add a ³⁄₁₆" turn-under allowance to each appliqué fabric piece.

Appliqué pieces to the background in numerical order.

Embroidery is shown in red.

Block 5

Appliqué Masterpiece: **Affairs of the Heart** *by Aie Rossmann*

Add a ³⁄₁₆" turn-under allowance to each appliqué fabric piece.
Appliqué pieces to the background in numerical order.
Embroidery is shown in red.

Block 6

Appliqué Masterpiece: **Affairs of the Heart** *by Aie Rossmann*

Add a ³⁄₁₆" turn-under allowance to each appliqué fabric piece.
Appliqué pieces to the background in numerical order.
Embroidery is shown in red.

Block 7

Add a ³⁄₁₆" turn-under allowance to each appliqué fabric piece.
Appliqué pieces to the background in numerical order.
Embroidery is shown in red.

Block 8

Add a ³⁄₁₆" turn-under allowance to each appliqué fabric piece.

Appliqué pieces to the background in numerical order.

Embroidery is shown in red.

Block 9

Appliqué Masterpiece: **Affairs of the Heart** *by Aie Rossmann*

Add a ³⁄₁₆" turn-under allowance to each appliqué fabric piece.
Appliqué pieces to the background in numerical order.
Embroidery is shown in red.

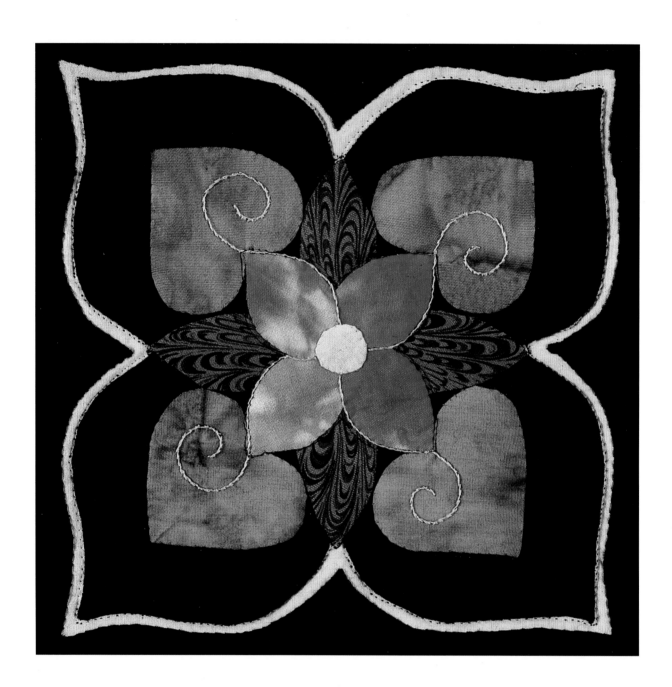

Block 10

Appliqué Masterpiece: **Affairs of the Heart** *by Aie Rossmann*

reverse appliqué first

Add a ³⁄₁₆" turn-under allowance to each appliqué fabric piece.
Embroidery is shown in red. Reverse appliqué is shown in gray.

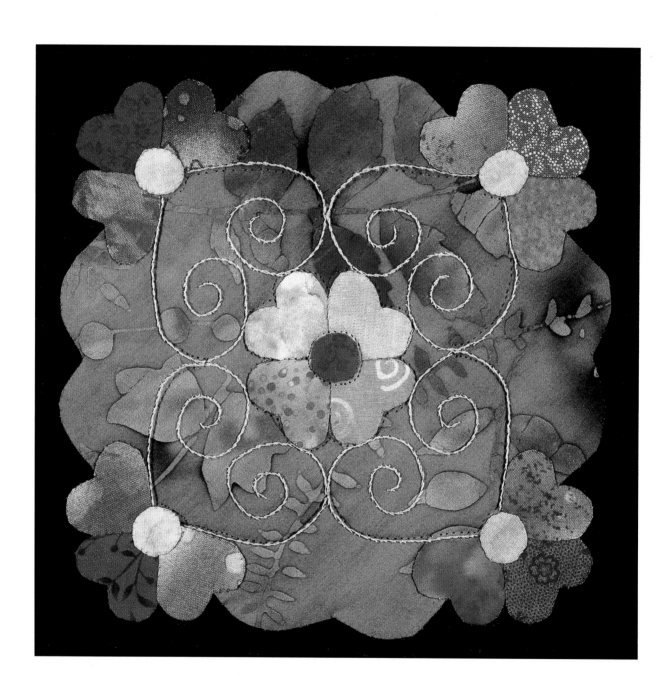

Block 11

Add a ³⁄₁₆" turn-under allowance to each appliqué fabric piece.

Appliqué pieces to the background in numerical order.

Embroidery is shown in red.

Block 12

Add a ³⁄₁₆" turn-under allowance to each appliqué fabric piece.
Appliqué pieces to the background in numerical order.
Embroidery is shown in red.

Block 13

Appliqué Masterpiece: **Affairs of the Heart** *by Aie Rossmann*

Add a ³⁄₁₆" turn-under allowance to each appliqué fabric piece.

Appliqué pieces to the background in numerical order.

Embroidery is shown in red.

Block 14

Appliqué Masterpiece: *Affairs of the Heart* *by Aie Rossmann*

Add a ³⁄₁₆" turn-under allowance to each appliqué fabric piece.
Appliqué pieces to the background in numerical order.
Embroidery is shown in red.

Block 15

Add a 3⁄16" turn-under allowance to each appliqué fabric piece.
Appliqué pieces to the background in numerical order.
Embroidery is shown in red.

Block 16

Appliqué Masterpiece: **Affairs of the Heart** *by Aie Rossmann*

Add a 3/16" turn-under allowance to each appliqué fabric piece.
Appliqué pieces to the background in numerical order.
Embroidery is shown in red.

Block 17

Add a ³⁄₁₆" turn-under allowance to each appliqué fabric piece.

Appliqué pieces to the background in numerical order.

Embroidery is shown in red.

Block 18

Add a ³⁄₁₆" turn-under allowance to each appliqué fabric piece.

Appliqué pieces to the background in numerical order.

Embroidery is shown in red.

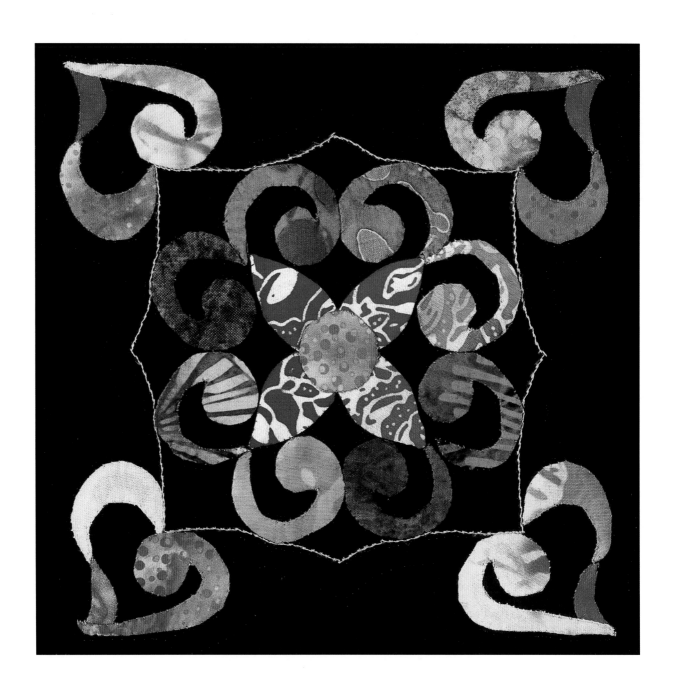

Block 19

Add a ³⁄₁₆" turn-under allowance to each appliqué fabric piece.
Appliqué pieces to the background in numerical order.
Embroidery is shown in red.

Block 20

Add a ³⁄₁₆" turn-under allowance to each appliqué fabric piece.
Appliqué pieces to the background in numerical order.
Embroidery is shown in red.

Block 21

Add a ³⁄₁₆" turn-under allowance to each appliqué fabric piece.

Appliqué pieces to the background in numerical order.

Embroidery is shown in red.

Block 22

Appliqué Masterpiece: **Affairs of the Heart** *by Aie Rossmann*

Add a ³⁄₁₆" turn-under allowance to each appliqué fabric piece.
Appliqué pieces to the background in numerical order.
Embroidery is shown in red.

Block 23

Add a ³⁄₁₆" turn-under allowance to each appliqué fabric piece.

Appliqué pieces to the background in numerical order.

Embroidery is shown in red.

Block 24

Appliqué Masterpiece: **Affairs of the Heart** *by Aie Rossmann*

Add a ³⁄₁₆" turn-under allowance to each appliqué fabric piece.

Appliqué pieces to the background in numerical order.

Embroidery is shown in red.

Block 25

Add a ³⁄₁₆" turn-under allowance to each appliqué fabric piece.

Appliqué pieces to the background in numerical order.

Embroidery is shown in red.

Block 26

Appliqué Masterpiece: **Affairs of the Heart** *by Aie Rossmann*

Add a ³⁄₁₆" turn-under allowance to each appliqué fabric piece.

Appliqué pieces to the background in numerical order.

Embroidery is shown in red.

Block 27

Appliqué Masterpiece: **Affairs of the Heart** *by Aie Rossmann*

Add a ³⁄₁₆" turn-under allowance to each appliqué fabric piece.

Appliqué pieces to the background in numerical order.

Embroidery is shown in red.

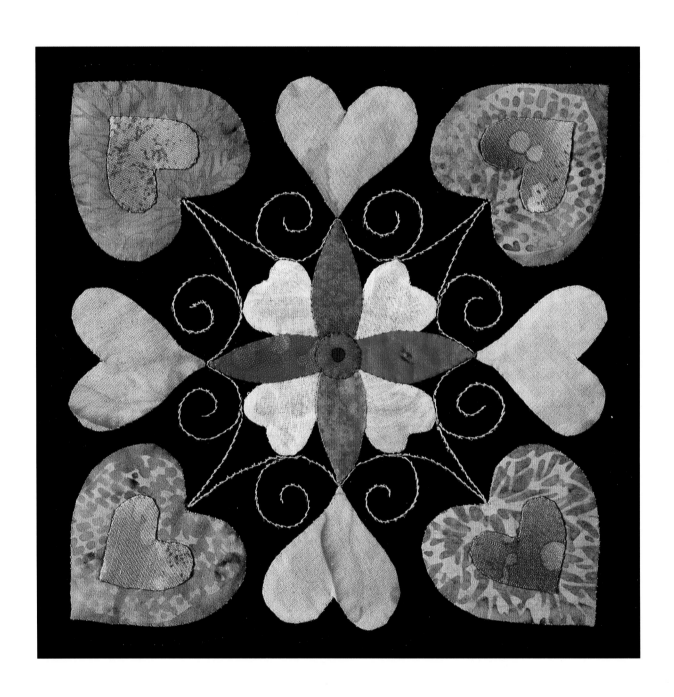

Block 28

Appliqué Masterpiece: **Affairs of the Heart** *by Aie Rossmann*

Add a ³⁄₁₆" turn-under allowance to each appliqué fabric piece.

Appliqué pieces to the background in numerical order.

Embroidery is shown in red.

Block 29

Add a ³⁄₁₆" turn-under allowance to each appliqué fabric piece.

Appliqué pieces to the background in numerical order.

Embroidery is shown in red.

Block 30

Add a ³⁄₁₆" turn-under allowance to each appliqué fabric piece.
Appliqué pieces to the background in numerical order.
Embroidery is shown in red.

Block 31

Appliqué Masterpiece: **Affairs of the Heart** *by Aie Rossmann*

Add a ³⁄₁₆" turn-under allowance to each appliqué fabric piece.

Appliqué pieces to the background in numerical order.

Embroidery is shown in red.

Block 32

Appliqué Masterpiece: **Affairs of the Heart** *by Aie Rossmann*

Add a ³⁄₁₆" turn-under allowance to each appliqué fabric piece.

Appliqué pieces to the background in numerical order.

Embroidery is shown in red.

Block 33

Add a ³⁄₁₆" turn-under allowance to each appliqué fabric piece.

Appliqué pieces to the background in numerical order.

Embroidery is shown in red.

Block 34

Appliqué Masterpiece: **Affairs of the Heart** *by Aie Rossmann*

Add a ³⁄₁₆" turn-under allowance to each appliqué fabric piece.

Appliqué pieces to the background in numerical order.

Embroidery is shown in red.

Block 35

Appliqué Masterpiece: **Affairs of the Heart** *by Aie Rossmann*

Add a ³⁄₁₆" turn-under allowance to each appliqué fabric piece.

Appliqué pieces to the background in numerical order.

Embroidery is shown in red.

Block 36

Appliqué Masterpiece: Affairs of the Heart *by Aie Rossmann*

Add a ³⁄₁₆" turn-under allowance to each appliqué fabric piece.

Appliqué pieces to the background in numerical order.

Embroidery is shown in red.

Border Patterns

Corner Heart

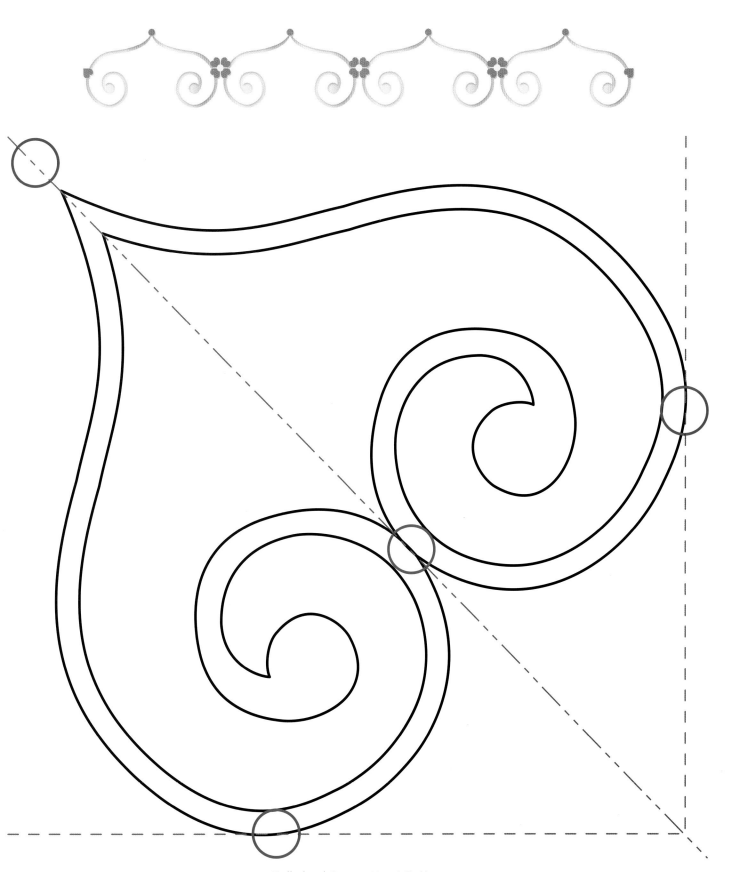

Full-sized Corner Heart Pattern

Appliqué the design as described on pages 15–16.

Appliqué the circles after all the appliqué is complete.

Section A

Border Scroll

Appliqué Masterpiece: **Affairs of the Heart** *by Aie Rossmann*

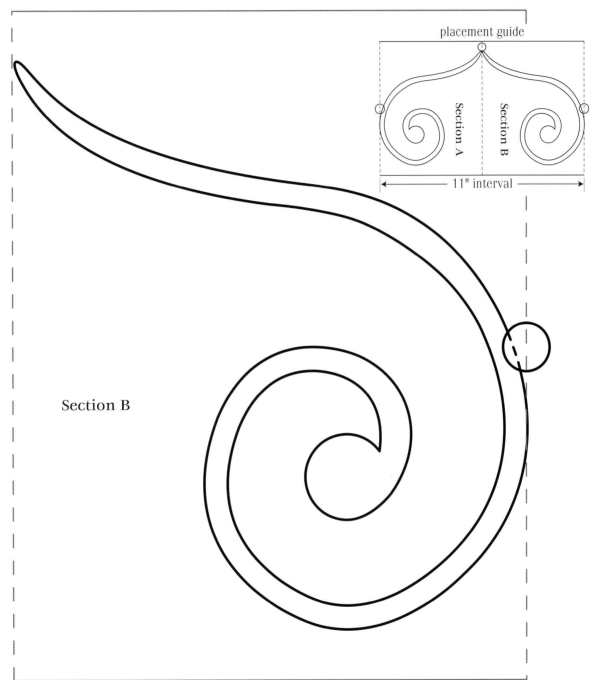

placement guide

Section A

Section B

← 11" interval →

Section B

Full-sized Scroll Pattern
Connect the patterns on pages 92 and 93 where indicated to complete the
11″ border motif. Appliqué the design as described on pages 14–15.
Appliqué the circles after all reverse appliqué is complete.

Hand Appliqué Books

Following is a list of the author's favorite hand appliqué reference books:

Pearson, Nancy. *Floral Appliqué.* Saddle Brook, New Jersey: Quilt House Publishing, 1994.

Docherty, Margaret. *Appliqué Masterpiece: Little Brown Bird Patterns.* Paducah, Kentucky: American Quilter's Society, 2000.

Campbell, Patricia B. and Mimi Ayars, Ph.D. *The Best of Jacobean Appliqué.* Paducah, Kentucky: American Quilter's Society, 2000.

Sienkiewicz, Elly. *Fancy Appliqué: 12 Lessons to Enhance Your Skills.* Lafayette, California: C&T, 1999.

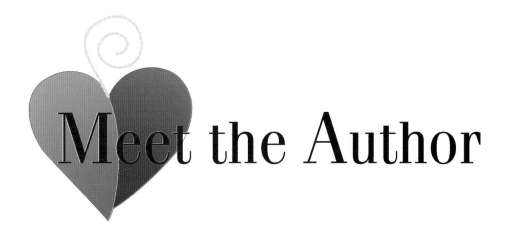

Meet the Author

An architect by trade, Aie (pronounced like a long A) is also skilled at drawing quilt designs. She began quilting while taking a break from her professional career to raise a family. Originally from Myanmar, formerly called Burma, Aie brings Southeast Asian influence to many of her designs and color schemes. The most recognizable aspects about the quilts she makes are their stylized, scrolled designs appliquéd in bright colors on a dark background. Her greatest source of inspiration is from ancient Burmese temple murals, which she studied as design motifs while earning a degree in architecture.

Design is Aie's favorite part of quiltmaking and she has created numerous original appliqué patterns. She started her own pattern business in 1999 and has published original designs under her *Lotusland's* label. The most rewarding aspect of quiltmaking for Aie is having a finished project. Even if the pattern is not published, she likes to see her ideas take life in the form of quilts.

A resident of Calgary, Canada, Aie teaches both needle-turn and machine appliqué internationally at quilt shops and retreats. Her patterns are available on the Internet at http://www.lotuslands.ab.ca. She can be reached by e-mail at aie@lotuslands.ab.ca.

other AQS books

This is only a small selection of the books available from the American Quilter's Society. AQS books are known worldwide for timely topics, clear writing, beautiful color photos, and accurate illustrations and patterns. The following books are available from your local bookseller, quilt shop, or public library.

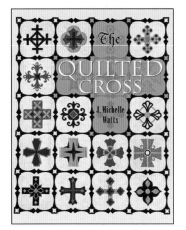

#6301   us$18.95

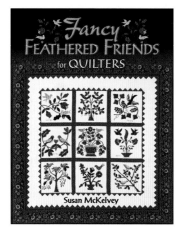

#6205   us$24.95

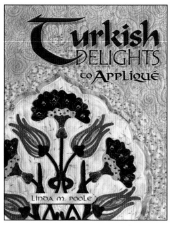

#6004   us$22.95

#6001   us$21.95

#6407   us$21.95

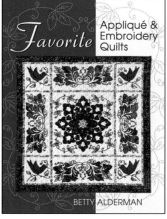

#6410   us$19.95

#6211   us$19.95

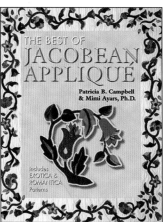

#5588   us$24.95

#5338   us$21.95

LOOK for these books nationally.
CALL or **VISIT** our Web site at

1-800-626-5420
www.americanquilter.com